Acting Edition

Bad Parent

by Ins Choi

Copyright © 2023 by Ins Choi
All Rights Reserved

BAD PARENT is fully protected under the copyright laws of the United States of America, the British Commonwealth, including Canada, and all member countries of the Berne Convention for the Protection of Literary and Artistic Works, the Universal Copyright Convention, and/or the World Trade Organization conforming to the Agreement on Trade Related Aspects of Intellectual Property Rights. All rights, including professional and amateur stage productions, recitation, lecturing, public reading, motion picture, radio broadcasting, television, online/digital production, and the rights of translation into foreign languages are strictly reserved.

ISBN 978-0-573-70983-8

www.concordtheatricals.com
www.concordtheatricals.co.uk

FOR PRODUCTION INQUIRIES

UNITED STATES AND CANADA
info@concordtheatricals.com
1-866-979-0447

UNITED KINGDOM AND EUROPE
licensing@concordtheatricals.co.uk
020-7054-7298

Each title is subject to availability from Concord Theatricals Corp., depending upon country of performance. Please be aware that *BAD PARENT* may not be licensed by Concord Theatricals Corp. in your territory. Professional and amateur producers should contact the nearest Concord Theatricals Corp. office or licensing partner to verify availability.

CAUTION: Professional and amateur producers are hereby warned that *BAD PARENT* is subject to a licensing fee. The purchase, renting, lending or use of this book does not constitute a license to perform this title(s), which license must be obtained from Concord Theatricals Corp. prior to any performance. Performance of this title(s) without a license is a violation of federal law and may subject the producer and/or presenter of such performances to civil penalties. Both amateurs and professionals considering a production are strongly advised to apply to the appropriate agent before starting rehearsals, advertising, or booking a theatre. A licensing fee must be paid whether the title(s) is presented for charity or gain and whether or not admission is charged. Professional/Stock licensing fees are quoted upon application to Concord Theatricals Corp.

This work is published by Concord Theatricals Corp.

No one shall make any changes in this title(s) for the purpose of production. No part of this book may be reproduced, stored in a retrieval system, scanned, uploaded, or transmitted in any form, by any means, now known or yet to be invented, including mechanical, electronic, digital, photocopying, recording, videotaping, or otherwise, without the prior written permission of the publisher. No one shall share this title(s), or any part of this title(s), through any social media or file hosting websites.

For all inquiries regarding motion picture, television, online/digital and other media rights, please contact Concord Theatricals Corp.

THIRD-PARTY MATERIALS USE NOTE

Licensees are solely responsible for obtaining formal written permission from copyright owners to use copyrighted third-party materials (e.g., incidental music not provided in connection with a performance license, artworks, logos) in the performance of this play and are strongly cautioned to do so. If no such permission is obtained by the licensee, then the licensee must use only original materials and materials that the licensee owns and controls. Licensees are solely responsible and liable for clearances of all third-party copyrighted materials, and shall indemnify the copyright owners of the play(s) and their licensing agent, Concord Theatricals Corp., against any costs, expenses, losses and liabilities arising from the use of such copyrighted third-party materials by licensees. For music, please contact the appropriate music licensing authority in your territory for the rights to any incidental music not provided in connection with a performance license.

IMPORTANT BILLING AND CREDIT REQUIREMENTS

If you have obtained performance rights to this title, please refer to your licensing agreement for important billing and credit requirements.

BAD PARENT was developed with the participation of Banff Playwrights Lab, Soulpepper Theatre Company, Vancouver Asian Canadian Theatre (vAct), and Prairie Theatre Exchange (PTE). Its rolling world premiere was jointly produced by vAct, Soulpepper Theatre, and PTE, and premiered in April 2022 at the Cultch's Historic Theatre in Vancouver, BC; followed by a run in September/October 2022 at the Michael Young Theatre in Toronto, ON; followed by a run in November 2022 at Prairie Theatre Exchange in Winnipeg, MB. The productions were directed by Meg Roe, with set and prop design by Sophie Tang, sound design and music production by Deanna H. Choi, costume design by Brenda McLean, and lighting design by Gerald King. The dramaturg was Thomas Morgan Jones, and the stage managers were Tracy Lynne Cann (Soulpepper) and Katie Hoopa (vAct, PTE). The cast was as follows:

NORAH / NORA . . . . Josette Jorge
CHARLES / DALE . . . . Raugi Yu

CHARACTERS

NORAH – Woman. She is married to Charles.

CHARLES – Man. He is married to Norah.

NORA – Woman. Played by the same actor playing Norah. She works as a nanny and speaks with a foreign accent.

DALE – Man. Played by the same actor playing Charles. He is Norah's colleague at work.

AUTHOR'S NOTES

An underline suggests some kind of emphasis.

(Offstage.) suggests physical distance between the actors but not necessarily "off the stage."

In the premiere production, Charles/Dale was played by a Taiwanese-Canadian actor and Norah/Nora was played by a Filipinx-Canadian actor. As such, Nora, the nanny, had a Filipinx accent but none of the other characters had accents.

In future productions, the casting is open to any ethnicities with two considerations: 1) The male actor must be of colour. 2) Nora, the nanny, must be from a culture that makes sense based on the casting of Norah, e.g. if the female actor has Zambian heritage and can speak with an authentic Zambian accent, then Nora the nanny can be from Zambia. Understandably, some script adjustments regarding references to Nora's country of origin will inevitably follow, e.g. song lyrics, lullaby, food references, etc. I'm interested in the nuances that'll emerge as a result of various diverse castings. All script adjustments must be submitted for approval to your Concord Theatricals' licensing representative.

Additionally, Concord Theatricals can provide licensees with reference tracks to interested licensees for "Nora's Filipino Food Truck" and "Run Run Norah." Please contact your licensing representative if you have questions.

To Poem and River, for growing me and Mommy so much.

Scene One

(**NORAH** and **CHARLES** *appear in a pool of light side by side, facing out to the audience together. Sometimes they're talking to each other and sometimes they're talking to the audience.*)

NORAH. Hello. Good evening. My name is Norah and this is my husband.

CHARLES. Hi everyone, my name is Charles and we first met…

NORAH. At one of his gigs.

CHARLES. I used to be in a band.

NORAH. He used to write songs.

CHARLES. I can still write songs.

NORAH. Actually, we first met at Kate's wedding. *(To him.)* Cuz it was at her wedding where you invited me to your gig.

CHARLES. Correct. Kate's her best friend.

NORAH. Not my best friend.

CHARLES. Technically, yes, that's where we first met but it was at my gig where I made the first real move, so –

NORAH. He sang a ballad from the stage looking right at me for the whole song.

CHARLES. Yes, and?

NORAH. It was a little embarrassing, truth be told.

CHARLES. Truth be told…her audience was all that mattered.

NORAH. Really.

CHARLES. Yes and still does. *(To her.)* What?

NORAH. But then after the show, he was too scared to say "hi," so I had to make the first move.

CHARLES. She wore this strapless black top and this miniskirt – she pretty much wore a tube interrupted by some skin.

NORAH. Yes, and?

CHARLES. How can I do anything when you're looking that hot?

NORAH. And now we have a baby boy.

CHARLES. But first we got married.

NORAH. And I got him a job.

CHARLES. She introduced me to Kate who got me the job.

NORAH. Kate produces TV shows. He's a music supervisor.

CHARLES. I find background music, that's all.

NORAH. He undersells himself and lacks ambition.

CHARLES. She used to be a production coordinator –

NORAH. Still am.

CHARLES. And now she's a mom.

NORAH. I'm on extended mat leave right now. We have a baby.

CHARLES. He's not a baby.

NORAH. His name is <u>Mountain</u>.

CHARLES. He's almost two.

NORAH. They think it's weird. His name.

CHARLES. She wanted to name him Donald.

NORAH. No, no, no, not Donald. Just Don.

CHARLES. The mountains were my way of finding my bearings where I grew up. And I thought what a great name for my son. *(To her.)* What?

NORAH. You said it was because of that wrestler from WWE.

CHARLES. That was a joke. Why would I name my son after a wrestler?

NORAH. Why you smiling then?

CHARLES. Why <u>you</u> smiling then?

NORAH. Cuz you're lying in front of them and kinda getting away with it.

CHARLES. Weird or not, that's his name now and he's amazing.

NORAH. He's so big for an eighteen-monther.

CHARLES. He can climb anything.

NORAH. He shouldn't climb anything at eighteen months.

CHARLES. That's what makes him so amazing. She said eighteen-monther.

NORAH. He thinks I'm not converting to years cuz I don't want him to grow up.

CHARLES. The boy not me. Her best friend, Kate, says her daughter is a thirty-eight-monther. What is that? Now we all gotta do math.

NORAH. Three years and two months.

CHARLES. See, we all understand that.

NORAH. Funny thing is we weren't even sure we wanted a baby.

CHARLES. We lacked experience.

NORAH. Not to mention the over-populated, under-resourced planet we'd be filling up.

CHARLES. We didn't even have a pet.

NORAH. But his parents and my dad weren't getting any younger and all of our friends were having babies.

CHARLES. So guess who got pregnant?

NORAH. First trimester was brutal. I never felt safe unless I was near a toilet.

CHARLES. She carried a plastic bag wherever she went.

NORAH. I threw up so much I got good at it.

CHARLES. People kept thinking she was looking for a dog.

NORAH. I could even aim my throw up.

CHARLES. But second and third trimester were fine.

NORAH. For you?

CHARLES. Until at the end she ballooned huge.

NORAH. My water broke while we were at his parents' place.

CHARLES. And there was this huge storm that night.

NORAH. So we couldn't go back to where we were living at the time.

CHARLES. She wanted a home birth.

NORAH. He googled what to do if your water breaks.

CHARLES. We had twenty-four hours.

NORAH. So we went to a nearby hospital

CHARLES. And the midwife met us there.

NORAH. The baby was sitting breech. They tried to turn it but nothing worked. I had to have a C-section.

CHARLES. And that was so scary.

NORAH. Must've been traumatic for you.

CHARLES. But it all worked out.

NORAH. Seven pounds two ounces.

CHARLES. And we just walked out of the hospital with it.

NORAH. They just let us go.

CHARLES. And then he didn't latch on right away. Something was wrong.

NORAH. Nothing was wrong with him.

CHARLES. No, something was wrong with you, remember?

NORAH. Postpartum, clogged nipples, I worry too much, take your pick.

CHARLES. She does.

NORAH. He doesn't worry enough.

CHARLES. But it all worked out.

NORAH. He eventually took.

CHARLES. Still taking.

NORAH. Yeah, that first year was pretty bumpy.

CHARLES. All of a sudden we were in charge of another life with the whole world watching.

NORAH. But now we're doing so much better. Right Charles?

CHARLES. Absolutely. So much.

(Lights snap out.)

Scene Two

(Lights snap in, and **CHARLES** *is in the midst of putting an IKEA bed together in their condo living room. He accidentally pinches his skin.)*

CHARLES. Ah! Dammit! *(To audience.)* I know. IKEA furniture, how hard can it be, right? And yet it is. Just want to get it done before Norah gets here. Cuz then she's gonna wanna help and lately we've had some IKEA furniture disasters. Not that the furniture is a disaster but the process of putting it together together usually ends disastrously. But it's also been a difficult time of adjusting, generally speaking. Like, you go from single to couple and that's one thing, but then you go from couple to trio and that's a totally different ballgame. So many moving parts, y'know? Norah's adjusting to being a new mom, I'm adjusting to being a new dad, and the boy's adjusting to being new. A word of caution for anyone here thinking of having kids: it's not easy, it's really hard, definitely amazing but there's a cost. And respectfully, it may not be for you. I don't mean to be insensitive, but honestly, I wish someone had told us that. We would've benefited huge just to hear it. Or like, when you're supposed to start feeling like a parent, y'know? I still feel like a kid. And I definitely don't feel like a dad. I look at other dads and they look like dads. People look at me and they think, "He can't even put a bed together, who gave him a baby?"

(Snap focus to **NORAH.***)*

NORAH. *(To audience, at the end of her rope.)* I don't know how other women do it. And I swore not to turn into my mother but guess what, here she is. *(Harshly.)* "Norah, you're strong, you're smart, stop crying and figure it out." That was my mother. She was this strong, independent woman that worked every day of her life and never asked for help. God, I miss work. I wish you could've seen me at work. When I used to work. I was good. People listened to me. I had status. I swear. But with this one, I've got nothing. My son. Mountain. Up there climbing on this ergonomically designed climbing apparatus no one knows how to use! *(To Mountain, exploding.)* Mountain! Get down here, right now! *(To audience.)* See? Nothing. He's not even looking at me. But he's not usually like this. I'm not usually like this. Charles gave him a Coke this morning. That's why he's like that making me like this! Coke Zero but still! Why do men do that? Make babies lick things, lemons, limes? Charles does that all the time. And then he complains he doesn't like him. Of course he doesn't. Why would you like someone who makes you lick things?

(Snap focus to **CHARLES.***)*

CHARLES. I just don't think he likes me very much. Is that weird? I mean, I made him. How can you not like the maker? Norah thinks it's cuz the boy can sense my annoyance with him every night when he sleeps with us. Yes. Every. Night. Starts in his crib, ends up in our bed. That's why I'm building this. *(Re: bed.)* It's not for me, it's for the boy. And no, he's not too young for it. Everyone develops at different rates. Plus, it was on sale, so. Well, it was in the "As-Is" section but there's nothing wrong with it. You start too nice, kids don't appreciate anything. They get used to it, expect it, demand it. I didn't have nice things when I was a kid, turned out pretty good. And my mom made do with a lot less for a lot longer than anyone should be able to. Seriously. She was a saint. She would mend our clothes so much it became more mend than clothe.

(Snap focus to **NORAH.***)*

NORAH. The reason my son doesn't listen to me is because Charles undermines my authority in front of him all the time. Yeah. Mocks me, questions me, so, of course this one doesn't take me seriously. It hasn't been exampled to him. Like father like son. We're supposed to be one voice, one sound, team parent, right? Wrong. Pulls that rug right out from under me each time and then throws me under the bus. No, that's not fair, it's not entirely Charles' fault. It's also his mother's.

*(Snap focus to **CHARLES**, then quickly back to **NORAH**.)*

I'm not kidding. Whenever we go over to his mother's house for dinner, she serves him hand and foot. Literally. She de-bones his fish for him and puts slippers on his feet. I'm not kidding. It's like a time capsule. And she still buys him underwear. What the hell is that? He's a frickin' grown-ass man. Buy your own underwear!

*(Snap focus to **CHARLES**.)*

CHARLES. I'm not saying I'm the world's greatest dad, far from it but at least with me, like, when he wakes up at night crying, let him cry it out, right? Let him learn how to soothe himself, build up that confidence, instead of just giving him the boob every time. She's the one insisting on breast-feeding <u>him</u>! At this rate, he's gonna be a weening teen! But that's all she does – a boob for this, a boob for that, yell a bunch of threats, no follow through! Case in point, the boy peed in the car today. Okay, so, she took him out earlier this morning to the playground, had a freak attack getting him down from something, so, to give her a break, I took him to IKEA with me at lunch. But before we went to IKEA, I took him out of his diapers. Yes, he's still in diapers! And we talk about all these things and then they just remain as is. That's our whole marriage. One big "As-Is" section at IKEA! Anyway, I took him out of his diapers to challenge him and guess what? He held his pee in all day and then peed in a urinal standing up. What?! Almost two and he's peeing like a little man. So proud of him. I got him an ice cream as a reward which he destroyed like a beast. And then on the way home –

> (**NORAH** *appears with a box of pizza and some groceries.* **CHARLES** *sees the audience see her.*)

What?

> (*Turns and sees her.*)

Scene Three

(It should seem as if there's a fourth wall all of a sudden.)

NORAH. Hey.

CHARLES. Hey.

NORAH. You okay?

CHARLES. Yeah. How was dinner?

NORAH. Good.

CHARLES. How's Kate doing?

NORAH. She's good too. I brought pizza. You hungry?

CHARLES. No. Not right now. Maybe later. Where'd you guys go?

(NORAH heads into the kitchen with some grocery bags.)

NORAH. *(Offstage.)* D'you want a drink?

CHARLES. *(Softly.)* Sure.

NORAH. *(Offstage.)* How was he?

CHARLES. Good. Sleeping now. *(Softly to the audience but not directly.)* On our bed. In our room. Not that I'm complaining. *(Regular.)* Don't know if I can be with him all afternoon tomorrow. Got some things to do. And my mom invited us for dinner Sunday night.

NORAH. *(Offstage.)* I'm having lunch with Kate. She asked about your availability by the way.

CHARLES. I'm too busy as it is.

NORAH. *(Offstage.)* That's why it's called work Charles.

CHARLES. I'm on pat leave.

NORAH. *(Offstage.)* We need the money.

CHARLES. I'm not making a career of being a music supervisor.

NORAH. *(Offstage.)* Then what are you making a career of?

CHARLES. Sunday night dinners at my mom's.

NORAH. *(Offstage.)* Aren't we already doing dinner to celebrate your brothers getting fired?

CHARLES. That's Saturday and they weren't fired, it's their new business venture.

NORAH. *(Offstage.)* Weren't they doing well with the real estate thing?

CHARLES. I'm talking about dinner on Sunday.

NORAH. *(Offstage.)* That's a lot of your family for one weekend.

CHARLES. Well, since you banished my mom –

NORAH. *(Entering with drink in hand.)* I didn't banish her. Just take Mountain to see her.

CHARLES. *(Facing away from her.)* She wants to see you.

NORAH. She wants to see you.

CHARLES. *(Teasing like, almost as if he's jealous that his mom prefers to see Mountain over him.)* She wants to see the baby.

NORAH. Exactly.

CHARLES. I'm saying "yes."

> (**CHARLES** *texts his mom.* **NORAH** *starts sipping the drink as her own throughout.)*

NORAH. Looks like you're building a bed, Charles.

CHARLES. It does look like that.

NORAH. You want some help?

CHARLES. Nope, almost done.

NORAH. I think we talked about this.

CHARLES. We did talk about this.

NORAH. And we decided to wait.

CHARLES. No, we didn't decide anything. We left it "As Is."

NORAH. This isn't "As Is."

CHARLES. Actually it is "As Is."

NORAH. You can't just –

CHARLES. I'm his dad. I can make a decision.

NORAH. Take it back.

CHARLES. Guess I can't.

NORAH. Unless it's for you, then, by all means.

CHARLES. I thought you said you had a good day?

NORAH. We already talked about this, left it "As Is" and then you go off on your own deciding for us? What is that?

CHARLES. You drag the boy into our bed every night deciding for us. What is that? So now that you've trained him to love beds more than cribs, I got him his own bed.

NORAH. That's not fair.

CHARLES. What's not fair is your addiction to sleeping with him. That's what's not fair. Stop sleeping with him. I'm your husband. Sleep with me. *(Beat.)* Is that my drink?

NORAH. No.

CHARLES. I thought you were making me a drink.

NORAH. I asked you.

CHARLES. And I said "sure."

NORAH. I didn't hear it.

CHARLES. *(Beat.)* Can I have a sip?

NORAH. *(Softly.)* Sure. *(He approaches.)* What?

CHARLES. Nothing.

NORAH. Don't drink it all.

> (**CHARLES** *takes the drink from* **NORAH**, *takes a sip and gives it back. He then gets the mattress and puts it on the bed and fits a sheet on it throughout this next section.*)

You want one?

CHARLES. No.

> *(Beat.)*

NORAH. Did you go to the drop-in centre?

CHARLES. He doesn't like it.

NORAH. What's wrong with the –

CHARLES. It's a bunch of Asian nannies on one side and white mommies on the other side judging each other for being terrible at their jobs. And I look like some kind of loser dad desperate to hook up with any of them.

NORAH. Which you wouldn't.

CHARLES. Because I'm not.

NORAH. I was gonna ask what's wrong with the bed? You said it's "As Is."

CHARLES. Nothing. Some scratches. It's a good enough bed.

NORAH. Did you take him to the park?

CHARLES. Yup.

NORAH. You put him on the swings?

CHARLES. Uh-huh.

NORAH. The baby swings or the big swings?

CHARLES. The big swings.

NORAH. Did he fall?

CHARLES. Nope. Once. A little.

NORAH. Guess he wasn't up to the challenge, then.

CHARLES. That's why it's called a challenge then.

NORAH. *(Mocking his grammar.)* "That's why it's called a challenge <u>then</u>"?

CHARLES. I was in a good mood before you got here.

NORAH. Me too. I even brought pizza.

CHARLES. You brought pizza because you feel bad about something like the last time you brought pizza. I was doing good, and then you got on me about, "Looks like you're building a bed, Charles. Did you go to the drop-in centre? Did you play with him at the park?"

NORAH. I didn't say –

CHARLES. Yes you did.

NORAH. I didn't –

CHARLES. Oh my god. We were right here. All that just happened. *(To audience.)* We all heard that, right?

NORAH. I didn't say, "Did you <u>play</u> with him at the park?" I said, "Did you <u>take</u> him to the park?" There's a big difference between "play" and "take" about which we've argued many times.

CHARLES. About which we've left "As Is" many times.

NORAH. Stop building the bed! (**CHARLES** *reaches for a screw and* **NORAH** *takes it.*) He needs the drop-in centre to build his social skills. He has no friends. And he's not like you, he doesn't want to be alone all the time.

CHARLES. Or maybe it's because –

NORAH. It's not about you, Charles! It's not about you all the time. Stop thinking about yourself for once. Did you feed him?

CHARLES. Yes.

NORAH. What did you feed him?

CHARLES. *(Sighs.)* Two meatballs, sixteen fries and he sipped a little gravy. Then what happened? Well, I'm glad you asked cuz then I had to take a dump. So what did I do? Interesting question cuz it was a real dilemma, thanks for asking. Well, I then proceeded to bring him into the stall with me while I took a dump. Win win. IKEA's got great washrooms and it was a great dump. Didn't even have to cut. Didn't even have to wipe but I did, as a good example to him, y'know? As the prime example of manhood. Then on the way home he peed in the car and I cleaned that up too. And now he's sleeping in our bed cuz you trained him to like beds. The end.

(**CHARLES** *returns to building the bed.*)

NORAH. How'd you know he peed in the car?

CHARLES. Cuz it was all over the car seat which I had to clean up, like I just said in my full report! No more questions.

NORAH. *(Slowly, figuring it out.)* But why would you have to clean up the car seat if he had his Pull-Ups on? Unless you took his Pull-Ups off to challenge him, which he failed by peeing in the car seat. Then, yes, you would've had to clean that up to cover your tracks. Which you did until just now when you outed yourself trying to make some kind of sarcastic point.

CHARLES. Yes, I did take his diapers off and guess what, he held his pee in all day and then peed standing up at a urinal like a little man.

NORAH. Proud of yourself?

CHARLES. No, I was proud of him. When's the last time you gave him an opportunity to do something you could be proud of for?

NORAH. *(Mocking his grammar.)* Proud of _for_?

CHARLES. Yes. Proud of _for_!

> (**NORAH** *marches towards their bedroom and* **CHARLES** *blocks her way.*)

NORAH. What are you doing?

CHARLES. What are _you_ doing?

NORAH. I wanna see him.

CHARLES. You're gonna wake him. Let him sleep.

NORAH. Charles?

CHARLES. Norah, it's not about you. It's not about you all the time. Stop thinking about yourself for once and think about him. What's good for him? What'll benefit him? Huh?

NORAH. A nanny.

CHARLES. *(Beat.)* What?

NORAH. A nanny's good for him. I hired a nanny. She starts tomorrow. I'm also starting tomorrow at my full-time job. Kate found something for me. That's what the pizza was for.

CHARLES. Seriously? What, no, that's, you – I'm here.

NORAH. But now you don't have to worry about it.

CHARLES. *(To audience.)* See that? She just made that decision and what, I gotta live with that? That's not fair. That's not fair right? She can't just do that.

NORAH. You just did that. *(To audience.)* He just did that with the bed.

CHARLES. *(To audience.)* But we talked about the bed.

NORAH. *(To audience.)* And when we talked about the bed, we left it "As Is." And what did he go and do? *(She gestures to the bed.)* This is not "As Is."

CHARLES. *(To her.)* Yes it is! *(To audience.)* But at least we talked about this. We didn't talk about that? That nanny came out of nowhere.

NORAH. *(To audience.)* Which makes his decision to go <u>against</u> our "leave it as is" decision, <u>worse</u> than my decision, which isn't going against any previously made decision.

CHARLES. *(To her.)* Because we didn't talk about it!

NORAH. *(To him.)* Exactly!

*(Mountain starts crying. They remain where they are. **NORAH** makes a slight move, then stops.)*

CHARLES. *(To audience.)* The boy has a challenge right now. An opportunity to man up. And what's she gonna do? She's gonna go pick him up, soothe him, feel necessary while robbing him of this chance to take one giant step towards mankind. *(To **NORAH**.)* Let him cry it out. He needs this to become a man.

NORAH. And how would you know? *(She goes to her son. Eventually the crying subsides.)*

CHARLES. *(To audience.)* She did banish her though. Well, my mom feels like she's been banished. And he's gonna need a bed at some point, so technically, this is an early purchase. *(Beat. Re: bed.)* Well, I did make it…so might as well.

(He gets into the bed to sleep. Lights fade out.)

Scene Four

(It's the following morning. **CHARLES** *is asleep in the bed he made for Mountain.* **NORA** *enters, singing a lullaby*. She speaks with a thick foreign accent.* **CHARLES** *rustles awake.)*

CHARLES. Norah?

NORA. Yes?

CHARLES. Norah?

NORA. Yes?

CHARLES. *(Seeing her.)* Oh. Hello.

NORA. Good morning.

CHARLES. You're not my wife.

NORA. No, sir. My name is Nora. I am the nanny.

CHARLES. Oh. Right. Your name is Norah?

NORA. Yes, sir.

CHARLES. My wife's name is Norah.

NORA. Yes sir.

CHARLES. That's quite a coincidence.

NORA. Ma'am took it as a sign that it was meant to be. But I am very good at my job and have wonderful reference letters if you have any cause for concern.

CHARLES. Who's Ma'am?

---

* A license to produce *Bad Parent* does not include a performance license for any third-party or copyrighted music. Licensees should create an original composition or use music in the public domain. For further information, please see the Music and Third-Party Materials Use Note on page iii.

NORA. Your wife, sir.

CHARLES. Where is she?

NORA. She went to work, sir.

CHARLES. Well, nice to meet you Norah. My name is Charles.

NORA. Nice to meet you too sir.

CHARLES. Might've been nice if Ma'am gave me the heads-up before you got here, don't you think? You don't have to answer that.

NORA. *(Beat.)* Would you like some breakfast in your bed sir?

CHARLES. Uh, sure.

> (**NORA** *exits to the kitchen.* **CHARLES** *puts on his pants and tidies up a bit.*)

It's not my bed. It's for the boy. This isn't how we usually...*(Beat.)* N-O-R-A-H?

NORA. *(Offstage.)* Pardon sir?

CHARLES. The spelling of your name? N-O-R-A-H?

NORA. *(Offstage.)* Without the "H," sir.

CHARLES. My wife has the "H."

NORA. *(Offstage.)* Yes sir.

CHARLES. I think Norah Ephron has the "H" too.

NORA. *(Offstage.)* I disagree, sir.

CHARLES. Do you know who I'm talking about?

NORA. *(Offstage.)* The Hollywood director of *Harry Met Sally, You've Got Mail, Sleepless in Seattle.*

CHARLES. Yes you do.

NORA. *(Offstage.)* Norah Jones has the "H" but not Nora Ephron. Nora Daza also does not have the "H."

CHARLES. You sure know your Noras, Nora.

NORA. *(Offstage.)* Thank you, sir.

CHARLES. Who's Nora Daza?

NORA. *(Offstage.)* She is a famous Filipino cook. She learn how to cook from Julia Childs.

CHARLES. Julia Childs?

NORA. *(Offstage.)* From the movie, *Julie & Julia* written and directed by Nora Ephron. Without the "H."

CHARLES. I take it my son is around here somewhere?

NORA. *(Offstage.)* He is taking a nap in his room.

CHARLES. In his room?

NORA. *(Offstage.)* Yes sir, in his crib. I transferred him to there.

> (**CHARLES** *can't believe it, goes to check. He returns dumbfounded as* **NORA** *re-enters with a tray of food.*)

CHARLES. How'd you do that?

NORA. I did not know what kind of groceries you had so –

CHARLES. No, how'd you get the boy to sleep in his crib? He hates cribs.

NORA. I am very good at my job, sir. Breakfast?

CHARLES. *(Taking the plate.)* Where'd you get this?

NORA. I did not know what kind of groceries you had, so, I brought it from home.

CHARLES. You cooked this?

NORA. Yes sir.

CHARLES. By yourself?

NORA. Yes sir.

CHARLES. *(As he eats some.)* What is it?

NORA. It is a traditional Filipino breakfast. Beef steak, fried egg, vegetables and garlic rice.

(**CHARLES** *abruptly stops eating.*)

What is wrong, sir? Are you allergic to something?

CHARLES. Pollen in the spring. This is amazing.

NORA. Thank you sir.

CHARLES. Wow. This is… Oh my God. Is this a regular Filipino breakfast?

NORA. Well, it is a traditional Filipino breakfast but because I am a good cook, I wouldn't call it "regular."

CHARLES. This is incredible. You could open a restaurant with this.

NORA. You really think so?

CHARLES. Definitely. Or at least a food truck. You don't know how good this is, do you?

NORA. My father and his brothers were very good cooks. Our family was known for our cooking. Even my children can cook very well. So, yes, I do know.

CHARLES. How many kids do you have?

NORA. Two boys. Back home. I'm working to bring them over one day.

CHARLES. Huh.

NORA. *(Intrigued.)* Do you really think a food truck could work, sir?

CHARLES. Oh, yeah, for sure.

NORA. But isn't it expensive?

CHARLES. Yeah but you'd make it all back in the first year, easy. I mean, I could market the hell out of this and if Ma'am set up the business side, bam, done. Wow! I can't get over how good this is!

NORA. Thank you, sir.

CHARLES. Can you – makes me feel a little funny when you call me "sir."

NORA. Your wife doesn't mind me calling her "Ma'am."

CHARLES. Of course she doesn't.

(NORA blurts out a laugh.)

Call me Charles.

NORA. Okay. Charles.

CHARLES. *(Correcting her pronunciation.)* Charles.

NORA. Charles.

CHARLES. Do you want help with your pronunciation? I just assumed you would but that's kinda –

NORA. Yes, it is. But, yes, I do. So…thank you? *(Sounds like "Dank you.")*

CHARLES. *(Correcting her pronunciation.)* Thhhank you.

NORA. Thhhank you.

CHARLES. You're welcome.

(They exchange smiles.)

NORA. Why don't you get refreshed Mr. Charles. *(NORA takes the plate.)* I can take that from you.

CHARLES. Oh, I'm not, wait, let me just… Don't throw that out, I'm gonna finish it.

NORA. *(Leaving.)* If you think this is good, wait 'til you taste my chicken Adobo.

CHARLES. *(Calling after her.)* See? Where can I go for chicken Adobo? Nora's…Filipino Food Truck! *(To himself.)* Nora's Filipino Food Truck. *(Records it on his phone.)* Nora's Filipino Food Truck.

(Singing*, figuring out the tune and the lyrics.)

CHARLES.
WHERE CAN I GO FOR CHICKEN ADOBO?

(Speaking.)

No.

(Singing.)
WHERE CAN YOU GO FOR CHICKEN ADOBO?
WHERE DO YOU GO FOR CHICKEN ADOBO?
WHERE DOES ONE GO FOR CHICKEN ADOBO?

*(Snap focus to **NORAH**.)*

---

* A license to produce *Bad Parent* does not include a performance license for any third-party or copyrighted music. Licensees should create an original composition or use music in the public domain. For further information, please see the Music and Third-Party Materials Use Note on page iii.

Scene Five

NORAH. *(To audience, joyous.)* Work. Work. I love work! I love work so much! I forgot how much I love work! At work, everyone's an adult, everyone can feed themselves, clean themselves and no one's crying. Usually. And we talk about things, adult things, adult issues, adult movies – that's not what I meant. And when I go home I love being with my son. It's perfect! I felt a little guilty the first day, but then I got over it really quickly. And then I felt guilty for how quickly I got over it but then I got over that really quickly too. And I have a desk! My desk, with only my things on it. I love my desk. At work? It all works. At home? With Charles? *(A tad of malice.)* I don't even have a desk!

(Snap focus to **CHARLES**. *He is putting a mic on a mic stand.)*

CHARLES. *(To audience.)* Y'know what she does? Ms. Nora, the nanny? She tells the boy, that I'm his dad. And that he's my son and that a son's job is to listen to his dad. She tells him that all the time. Constantly reminding him, re-enforcing it – and then my son sees her laugh at my jokes – my son sees me correcting her pronunciation – he's learning from her example what it looks like to respect me. I know, it's kinda weird cuz I'm her employer, so it's a bit, but she makes me look so good. That's my point. Better, even. And she cooks, she cleans, she's so nice to me. Come on! This. Works!

(Snap focus to **NORAH**.*)*

NORAH. *(Trying to figure out this mystery in front of and with the audience.)* See, the thing about it is, at work, people know what to expect before they're even hired. And if someone isn't meeting that expectation, they're fired, right? Plain and simple. And if someone exceeds that expectation, they're given a raise or promoted. But in a marriage... I mean, what's a raise or a promotion?! What's the job description? If anything, it's longer hours, less benefits, and you can't give a performance assessment without him blowing up cuz he's not clear on who the boss is!

(**DALE** *enters with some papers and a pen.*)

DALE. Hi. Are you Norah?

NORAH. Yes. And you are?

DALE. Dale. We've corresponded.

NORAH. Dale, from accounting.

DALE. Yes.

NORAH. Good to put a face to an email.

DALE. And a number. How are you settling in?

NORAH. Good. Finally learned how that coffee contraption works.

DALE. You're a quick study then. I still don't know. (**NORAH** *chuckles.*) But don't get too used to it. A new one's bound to be here next month.

NORAH. Kate's predilection for new toys?

DALE. Oh, so you know Kate well.

NORAH. *(Chuckles.)* We go back a little.

DALE. Mind if I get your autograph here and here?

NORAH. Oh, thought this was a friendly visit.

DALE. Can't it be both?

NORAH. *(Signing.)* I'm kidding.

DALE. You just had a baby, right?

NORAH. *(Teasing him, inferring that he's commenting on her figure.)* Is it that obvious?

DALE. Oh, no, sorry, you look fantastic without any caveats or provisos.

NORAH. Thank you. Yes I did. He's an eighteen-monther.

DALE. I have a twenty-six-monther and a forty-eight-monther. Boy?

NORAH. Yeah. Yours? Girl, boy?

DALE. Good guess. *(Beat.)* Well, thank you for this, *(Re: signing forms.)* great to have met you in the flesh, and next time I'll have no reason to speak to you.

NORAH. Oh! Uh, what happened to the previous production coordinator? I didn't want to pry.

DALE. Nothing scandalous. She was good, but maybe just not a good fit?

NORAH. Gotcha.

DALE. *(Leaving.)* Okay, bye for now.

NORAH. Bye. *(Ecstatic.)* See that?! Did everyone just see all of that fun banter between two adults with no fighting?! This! Works!

*(Snap focus to **CHARLES**.)*

CHARLES. *(To audience.)* Mic check. Testing one two three. Testing one two three.

*(**NORA** enters.)*

NORA. *(Excited, impressed.)* Wowee!! Mr. Charles, this is such a fancy place! I can not believe all this is happening. I have never been in a recording studio before.

CHARLES. Don't let any of this intimidate you. If we make a mistake, we can always do it again. No problem.

NORA. Thank you Mr. Charles for believing in me.

CHARLES. You're welcome. *(Gives her some headphones.)* Now, put these on your pretty ears and let's try one.

NORA. Mr. Charles, even if this does not work out –

CHARLES. What?

NORA. Even if we do not get a food truck in the end, it still means a lot to me.

CHARLES. Well, nothing's happened yet and trust me, it'll work. Ready?

NORA. Yes.

CHARLES. Just like we practiced okay?

NORA. I will not let you down, Mr. Charles. Cue the music.

CHARLES. *(To the booth.)* Alright, we're good to go.

(Fun, cute, upbeat recorded music.*)

NORA & CHARLES. *(Singing with harmony, they should sound really good together.)*
WHERE DO YOU GO WHEN YOU WANT CHICKEN ADOBO
AFTER THAT BIG GIG WHERE CAN YOU GET SISIG
WE'RE ON THE ROAD, NOT FAR FROM YOU
WE'RE LIKE MEALS ON WHEELS BUT WITH FILIPINO FOOD

NORA'S FILIPINO FOOD TRUCK
NORA'S FILIPINO FOOD TRUCK
NORA'S FILIPINO FOOD TRUCK

IN YOUR NEIGHBOURHOOD WITH FILIPINO FOOD.
IT'S GOOD LUCK TO EAT AT NORA'S FILIPINO FOOD TRUCK!

(They make a connection. Lights snap out.)

---

*A license to produce *Bad Parent* does not include a performance license for any third-party or copyrighted music. Licensees should create an original composition or use music in the public domain. For further information, please see the Music and Third-Party Materials Use Note on page iii.

Scene Six

(A soft clock is heard ticking in the condo as lights fade in to reveal **CHARLES** *trying to disassemble the bed. This could take a moment.* **NORAH** *enters the condo with all of her stuff from work. They see each other. There's a moment for someone to break the ice. She heads for the washroom.)*

CHARLES. *(To audience.)* Sure, I guess I could've said "hey" just now. Made the first move. But there was nothing stopping her from saying "hey" either. *(Beat.)* That was petty. I know. But Norah's very confident. Even when she's wrong, she's confident. I'm not. I could be a hundred percent right and my level of confidence is at par with her level of confidence when she's a hundred percent wrong. And she knows that. My brothers are super confident too. Like my dad. No hesitation, never. It's because he challenged them all the time. Everything was some kind of training or a contest – pushups, chinups, increasing pain thresholds, y'know? I was younger and kinda chubby, so, my mom would keep me away from all that. But when she wasn't around, they'd jump on me, no holds barred. I mean, it was fun too. Like, they'd throw me around and try wrestling moves on me. They'd put me in a figure four leg lock, and squeeze my belly out, yelling, "Let's see that fat pussy!" I hated that so much. And if that wasn't bad enough, one of them would then keep me pinned down while the other *(Enacting it.)* slid his pants and underwear down then sit on my face and fart. Like, my nose would be right up there between his butt cheeks. I know, so gross. But not as gross as it was humiliating when they'd do that to me in front of their friends. Why would they do that? And I'd just take it and laugh along. And then my dad would get so mad. At me, for not fighting back, but I couldn't cuz I wouldn't even think about it. I'd just freeze in a panic.

*(**NORAH** enters. They see each other. He goes on his phone. She begins folding laundry and picking up toys and clothes off the floor. **CHARLES** becomes aware that he's not helping to clean up in front of the audience and starts cleaning. **NORAH** picks up her pace, and it becomes a race to see who can clean more in front of the audience. As **CHARLES** is about to "win":)*

NORAH. Are you free on the fifteenth?

CHARLES. Huh?

NORAH. The fifteenth, are you available in the evening?

CHARLES. Oh, uh, hold on. *(He checks.)* No, I'm not.

NORAH. What about the twenty-second?

CHARLES. *(Checks his phone.)* I dunno, that's uh, too far to tell.

NORAH. What does that mean?

CHARLES. It's too far in the future to plan for. So, something else might come up between now and then.

NORAH. Then that something else will have to be planned around the thing you already planned. Either you plan for something and that's the thing you're doing or you don't do anything cuz you're always waiting for something better to come up.

*(**CHARLES** leaves.)*

Where you going? Where are you going?!

*(Door slams. **NORAH** gestures aggressive frustration. She flips her lid.)*

That's not on me! I tried. You saw. You were here. I made the first move. It's not my fault he has difficulty planning ahead! *(Beat.)* What? You think I'm in the wrong? Put your hand up if you think I was in the wrong just now.

(If people raise their hands, she can respond with something in the vein of, "Wow, that was pretty fast," or, "Oh. Okay then." And if people don't raise their hands, she can respond with, "Great. Thank you." And then:)

But just so you know, there's a whole lot more to him than what you've seen or what he's told you. I mean, he presents as this progressive, sensitive, modern man with contemporary values but as soon as Mountain was born, all of a sudden, he became, I dunno, not the man I married. Yeah, all of a sudden, he took issue with me not taking his last name. Can you believe that? He said cuz Mountain would always question who his real mother was if our last names didn't match. So ridiculous. He changed, that's all I'm saying. Like, he once wrote me a song. Yeah. He did. I was running this marathon after my mother died. I felt like doing something difficult to grieve, y'know? and it was. Super hard. And Charles traveled to different spots along the route holding up a sign yelling the song to me, "Run Norah Run". He was cheering for me and it felt so good running for him. I mean, I was running for breast cancer but his audience was all that mattered. So it's not like, I mean – No. No! Charles has to up his game! And the thing is, he can. Some men can't. I get that. Some men max out down here but when Charles mans up, Oh my God! I catch a glimpse of the power couple we were intended to be and just...! You should see him when he's planning a vacation. He takes initiative, he researches, compares, and then knows exactly what he wants and gets it. He spends more time planning for the vacation than being on the vacation. He loves hunting for a great deal. You should see him at a buffet. He eats so much, he makes money.

(Lights snap out.)

Scene Seven

*(Baby cries for a bit, then fades. Lights fade in to reveal **CHARLES** irritatedly disassembling the bed further. **NORA** enters with her plate of samples.)*

NORA. What do you think?

CHARLES. Oh, thanks. Sure, maybe later.

NORA. *(Chuckling.)* These are the samples silly boy.

CHARLES. Samples for what?

NORA. *(Slowly.)* The samples for the food…for the food truck?

CHARLES. Oh, right. We're doing this now?

NORA. I can come back later.

CHARLES. *(Beat.)* No, it's okay. You're here, food's ready.

NORA. I'll come back.

CHARLES. No, let's do this now. This the chicken? *(She feeds him.)*

NORA. Mm-hm.

CHARLES. Oh, that's really good. This is the pork? *(She feeds him.)*

NORA. Yes.

CHARLES. Wow, that just melts in your mouth doesn't it? Holy. And this is the vegan? *(She feeds him.)*

NORA. Yes.

CHARLES. That tastes really vegan.

NORA. *(Playfully shoving him.)* Mr. Charles.

CHARLES. Does us no good for me to lie. I'm kidding. It's good. It's all good. Everything is approved. Great work.

NORA. Do you think we need a vegetarian option in addition to a vegan one? They are two different things but I would not want to give too many options to the customers. Makes it look like we are not good at anything or we do not know what we are good at.

CHARLES. Yup, gotta know what you're good at.

NORA. *(Beat.)* Have you talked to Ma'am?

CHARLES. No. Not yet. Communication seemed to be our problem, so we stopped communicating. There, problem solved. She can be a bit of a...

NORA. Ma'am is not that bad. *(Off his look.)* She's not.

CHARLES. She cut off my ponytail while I was sleeping once.

NORA. No, I don't believe you.

CHARLES. You don't believe she cut off my ponytail?

NORA. I don't believe you had a ponytail. Kidding.

CHARLES. Swear to god, just like that Leonard Cohen song.

NORA. Like Samson and Delilah.

CHARLES. Who?

NORA. From the Bible. God gives Samson secret power when his hair is long. Then he sleeps with Delilah and tells her his secret and she cuts off his hair while he is sleeping.

CHARLES. Yeah, that pretty much sums up what happened with us. *(He goes to his room. Offstage.)* Have you seen my shirt? The blue stretchy one that's not too stretchy but stretchy enough?

NORA. It is hanging in your closet on the left side. I found it crumpled up in the corner of Mountain's room.

CHARLES. *(Offstage.)* I knew I left it there.

NORA. You are welcome. *(Beat.)* When do you think you will be talking to Ma'am then?

CHARLES. *(Offstage.)* What's that?

NORA. When do you think you will be talking to Ma'am about the food truck?

CHARLES. *(Entering with the blue shirt on.)* Well, let me talk to her about it and I'll get back to you.

NORA. *(Cautiously.)* Do you no longer wish to do the food truck?

CHARLES. *(A tad irritated.)* What? Ms. Nora I gotta go. These things take time. I just sent in the application for the license and my business plan is almost finished. Would I have done that if I no longer wished to do the food truck? And it's not like there's a whole fleet of them waiting to beat us to the curb either.

NORA. I thought Ma'am was coming up with the business plan?

CHARLES. Anyone can come up with a business plan.

NORA. Mr. Charles, we need a real business plan –

CHARLES. I have a real one.

NORA. That will survive the scrutiny of a real bank loan application.

CHARLES. We don't need a bank loan application cuz we don't need a bank loan. We have savings.

NORA. And you will be investing in my food truck?

CHARLES. Our food truck. Yes.

NORA. When were you going to tell me about that?

CHARLES. After I spoke with Ma'am.

NORA. Running a business is more than writing a song.

CHARLES. Ms. Nora –

NORA. *(Stern.)* It is my cooking Mr. Charles! You cannot string me along without any consideration of what I think or how I feel. Why are you doing this alone? We are supposed to be doing this together.

CHARLES. We don't have to be doing this at all! I don't owe you anything. There, no more food truck, happy?

    (Long beat.)

NORA. I apologize Mr. Charles. I was out of line.

CHARLES. I didn't mean to raise my voice. We'll talk about it later, alright?

NORA. Yes.

CHARLES. Don't worry about it. I'll talk to Ma'am. We'll figure it out.

    (The rice cooker sounds. **NORA** *goes to it.* **CHARLES** *resumes disassembling the bed, during which he turns to the audience from time to time, unable to find the words. Snap focus to* **NORAH.***)*

Scene Eight

(**NORAH** *is at her office. She's reading the card attached to a box of chocolates.*)

NORAH. *(Reading, smiling.)* "Congrats on a seamless transition. Couldn't do this without your help. You make me better. Thank you. Signed, Kate."

(**DALE** *passes by and catches her attention.*)

Dale.

DALE. Hey.

NORAH. Want a chocolate?

DALE. Why? What do you want from me? (**NORAH** *chuckles.*) Sure. Thanks.

(*They both take one, cheers with it.*)

NORAH & DALE. Cheers.

(*They eat it. It's really good. They make sensual sounds.*)

DALE. Wow.

NORAH. Mm-hm.

DALE. Holy. It's a little embarrassing how much I'm enjoying this.

NORAH. I think I just got pregnant again.

DALE. *(Chuckles.)* You guys thinking of having another? Make a big brother out of a Mountain?

NORAH. Oh. No. We're one and done.

DALE. Yeah, that's good too. We'd be clear out of the woods by now.

NORAH. How do you mean?

DALE. Diapers, feedings, getting them to walk. All great and wonderful, but once they can wipe and feed themselves, the war is over.

NORAH. Yeah, that sounds about right. *(Beat.)* Hey, can we pretend we're closer than we are?

DALE. *(Taking a step closer.)* Now we don't have to pretend. Sorry. Dumb joke. (**NORAH** *smiles.*) What is it?

NORAH. *(Hesitant.)* Do you think I'm easy to work with?

DALE. Sure. Why?

NORAH. *(Sighs.)* My husband and I are in a rough spot.

DALE. Ah.

NORAH. Yeah, we've been in this rough spot since we had the baby. And I've come to the conclusion that it's more him than me.

DALE. Very mature of you.

NORAH. See, that's me at home. But here at work, I'm easy to work with, I'm amazing, according to you.

DALE. Not sure I said "amazing" –

NORAH. And I think it's because we have defined roles at work. We have a purpose here, y'know? A way to be evaluated.

DALE. Don't think I quite follow.

NORAH. Yeah, I don't think I quite follow either.

DALE. If it helps, my wife and I were in a rough patch way before the kids arrived. Actually, the kids made it so we didn't really have to talk to each other. I think that's why we had the second.

NORAH. And once they grow up and leave?

DALE. Well, if we keep having kids, we'll never have to figure things out.

NORAH. *(Chuckles.)* See? Why is this so easy?

DALE. *(Thinking while talking.)* Cuz we're pretty much strangers here presenting our best self?

NORAH. *(Thinking while talking.)* For a short amount of time.

DALE. *(Thinking while talking.)* So there's no history. No judgement.

NORAH. *(Thinking while talking.)* Cuz you don't really care about me.

DALE. *(Thinking while talking.)* Nor can you make me look bad.

NORAH. *(Thinking while talking.)* Nor do I want to.

DALE. *(Thinking while talking.)* Nor do you keep a record of all the wrongs I've done in my life.

NORAH. *(Thinking while talking.)* Nor are you a constant reminder of all the wrongs I've done in my life.

DALE. And love.

NORAH. Yeah. That's a pretty big one.

DALE. I don't love you. Sorry.

NORAH. No. I don't love you either. You could die tomorrow and of course I'd be sad but then I'd be thinking about lunch. *(They share a smile. There might be a slight impulse to kiss.)* Dale, I think you're easy to work with too.

DALE. Norah, I think...we deserve another one of those. *(Re: chocolates.)*

NORAH. *(Each taking one.)* Yes we do.

DALE. Thanks. *(Leaving.)* And at work, I have an office to go to! I don't have an office at home!

NORAH. I know! I don't even have a desk!

> *(She turns to the audience, unable to find the words. Snap focus to* **CHARLES.** *)*

Scene Nine

(**CHARLES** *has earbuds in and is listening to something. He sees the audience.*)

CHARLES. I'm listening to a voice memo of the last song I wrote. It was for Norah. She used to run marathons. *(Beat.)* Wanna hear it? *(Maybe there's one or two yeses.)* Doesn't sound like you do. Wanna hear it? *(Hopefully they cheer "yes".)* Okay then.

(*He pulls out his earbuds and we hear the song, "Run Run Norah," play over the PA.* It's soft and sounds like a voice recording. After it finishes:*)

Bit of a letdown. I know. But when I hear that, to me, it sounds like this.

(*This is* **CHARLES**' *fantasy. He hears the audience applause.*)

Not too big of an audience but not too small either. Maybe five hundred. *(Applause bumps up.)* Okay seven hundred. *(Applause bumps up.)* Okay a thousand max. *(Applause bumps up. He picks up a mic.)* And the bass kicks in right about now. *(Bass kicks in.)* And there's lights and smoke. *(Concert lights and smoke.)* And everyone's dancing and cheering and everyone knows the song and echoes the chorus.

RUN RUN NORAH *(Recorded audience responding to him: Run-run Norah.)*
RUN RUN NORAH *(Recorded audience responding to him: Run-run Norah.)*

---

*A license to produce Bad Parent *does not include a performance license for any third-party or copyrighted music. Licensees should create an original composition or use music in the public domain. For further information, please see the Music and Third-Party Materials Use Note on page iii.*

CHARLES.
> RUN RUN NORAH *(Recorded audience responding to him: Run-run Norah.)*
>
> RUN RUN NORAH *(Recorded audience responding to him: Run-run Norah.)*
>
> RUN NORAH RUN
>
> RUN AHEAD OF EVERYONE
>
> RUN TOWARDS THE SETTING SUN BEFORE IT HITS THE HORIZON
>
> RUN NORAH RUN
>
> RUN REAL FAST YOU'VE JUST BEGUN
>
> RUN FOR FUN DON'T BE OUTDONE BY ANY ONE
>
> RUN RUN NORAH *(RECORDED AUDIENCE RESPONDING TO HIM: RUN-RUN NORAH.)*
>
> RUN RUN NORAH *(RECORDED AUDIENCE RESPONDING TO HIM: RUN-RUN NORAH.)*
>
> RUN RUN NORAH *(RECORDED AUDIENCE RESPONDING TO HIM: RUN-RUN NORAH.)*
>
> RUN RUN NORAH *(Recorded audience responding to him: Run-run run!)*

(The song ends. Maybe the audience applauds. Maybe there's confetti. Lighting reverts back to normal condo lighting as before. **CHARLES** *is facing downstage, very still as if lost in thought.* **NORAH** *enters and puts a few bags down. She sees* **CHARLES**.*)*

NORAH. I want a divorce, Charles. (**CHARLES** *freezes.*)

I can't do this anymore.

I'm tired of it. All of it.

You take me for granted.

I'm not your mom.

I'm not the manager of us.

BAD PARENT

(Drone-like music begins with a slow transition in lighting. This is **NORAH**'s *fantasy.**)

It's not my job to do everything around here or to clean it all up. You're like a child. You don't help. I'm so tired of looking after you. This is supposed to be a partnership. We're supposed to be best friends. I don't know what we are anymore. I didn't sign up for this. Why can't we talk honestly without it turning into a fight every time? Huh? I hate this. It's not worth it!

(She starts trashing the place, screaming. And once she's done:)

Do you remember that time at the playground when that woman came up to me? She saw me bottle feeding Mountain and after learning I was using formula, she began to lecture me, listing all the benefits of breast feeding and what a horrible mother I was. She didn't even bother to find out my nipples were clogged and so painfully sore. She reamed me out for being a bad parent... And I froze, so scared, so ashamed, utterly destroyed. And you just sat there and did nothing.

(As she walks back to where she was when she entered, sound slowly fades as lighting gradually reverts back to normal condo lighting. She sees **CHARLES***. She then pulls a big cardboard box into the condo. The sound makes* **CHARLES** *turn.)*

CHARLES. Hey.

---

*A license to produce *Bad Parent* does not include a performance license for any third-party or copyrighted music. Licensees should create an original composition or use music in the public domain. For further information, please see the Music and Third-Party Materials Use Note on page iii.

Scene Ten

NORAH. *(Beat.)* Hey.

CHARLES. *(Beat.)* What's in the box?

NORAH. It's not a pizza. It's a desk.

CHARLES. Think the boy might be a little young for a desk.

NORAH. Everyone develops at different rates. It's for me. I need a desk at home. You okay with that?

CHARLES. You asking?

NORAH. Yeah.

CHARLES. But you already bought it.

NORAH. I could take it back. It wasn't from the "As-Is" section.

CHARLES. Sure.

NORAH. You got a letter.

> (**CHARLES** *takes the letter gently from her.* **NORAH** *settles her things and begins assembling the desk as he opens and reads the letter. It's the approved license for the food truck.*)

He asleep?

CHARLES. In his room.

NORAH. *(Beat. Cautiously.)* What do you think about us… going on a vacation with Mountain. Our first family vacation. Three or four days on a beach somewhere. Thought it might be good for us. Doesn't have to be expensive. Kate went to Costa Rica last year and learned how to surf. I dunno. At the very least it's a change of scenery, change of pace.

*(By now **CHARLES** is finished reading the letter.)*

CHARLES. Yeah. I think it's a great idea.

NORAH. Really?

CHARLES. It would be good for us and he flies free 'til he's two. I'll look into it.

NORAH. *(Smiles.)* Great.

CHARLES. *(Re: desk.)* Want some help?

NORAH. Sure.

(He helps her assemble the desk. This could take a moment.)

CHARLES. Ms. Nora's working out pretty well.

NORAH. Yeah, she's like the perfect mom, I hate her. Kidding. *(Beat.)* Why do you call her Ms. Nora?

CHARLES. I don't know. She calls me Mr. Charles *(They chuckle together.)* I don't know how that happened. *(Beat.)* Hey, remember how we used to talk about doing more with our money?

NORAH. My mother's money?

CHARLES. Meaningful investments, saving the planet, stuff like that?

NORAH. Yeah.

CHARLES. And, I don't know, Ms. Nora's such a great cook, I was thinking, y'know, after we come back from our Costa Rican family surfing vacation, maybe we could start a food truck or something like that.

NORAH. A food truck?

CHARLES. Yeah, like a real business venture. Nora's Filipino food truck.

NORAH. You mean like a real food truck?

CHARLES. Something for Ms. Nora and her kids she wants to bring over. It's her dream. She could make a simple menu, I'd do the marketing, you'd do all the business stuff, we'd split it fifty-fifty and we just got approved for the license so...

> (*He shows the letter. She takes it and reads it, surprised that it seems to already be underway.*)

I wrote a jingle for it. Ms. Nora's quite the singer.

NORAH. You wrote her a song?

CHARLES. The recording's not finished but you wanna hear it?

NORAH. Did you give her any money?

CHARLES. What?

NORAH. For the food truck. Did you give her any money?

CHARLES. What do you mean?

NORAH. How much money did you give her Charles?

CHARLES. Nothing. I didn't give her any money. That's why I'm – Why do you think I'm talking to you?

NORAH. Did you sleep with her?

CHARLES. No. Did you sleep with her?

NORAH. This isn't a good idea.

CHARLES. What just happened? Why?

NORAH. Cuz it isn't.

CHARLES. You didn't even –

NORAH. It's a bad idea, Charles. I have no time and writing a song isn't marketing.

CHARLES. Okay, why don't we just...Let's talk about this later.

> (**CHARLES** *reaches for the license.* **NORAH** *keeps it away.*)

Can I have it back?

NORAH. I'm not finished with it.

CHARLES. Give it to me.

NORAH. I'm not finished reading it.

CHARLES. Why you reading it when it's a bad idea? Give it to me.

NORAH. No.

> (**CHARLES** *manhandles her and snatches the license out of her hand.*)

Hey!

CHARLES. It's mine.

> (**CHARLES** *puts the letter away.*)

NORAH. Apologize to me right now!

CHARLES. Don't yell at me!

NORAH. Apologize.

CHARLES. You didn't let go of my letter.

NORAH. I wasn't finished reading it.

CHARLES. You were gonna rip it up.

NORAH. You grabbed it out of my hand.

CHARLES. You grab a lot of things.

NORAH. Apologize to me right now.

CHARLES. Then you apologize to me right now!

NORAH. For what? For having an opinion? For thinking your stupid idea is a stupid idea?

CHARLES. For cutting off my ponytail. *(Beat.)* Did you or did you not cut off my ponytail while I was sleeping?

NORAH. Why are you still thinking about that?

CHARLES. Why are you so quick to forget it?

NORAH. That was three years ago.

CHARLES. *(To audience.)* See, told you she did it. She stole my power.

NORAH. You told them about that?

CHARLES. You tell them about a lot of things!

NORAH. *(Beat. To audience.)* His mother and I never got along. She always thought I wasn't good enough for her little prince. But she hated his ponytail more than she hated me.

CHARLES. She didn't hate it.

NORAH. So, as a peace offering to her, I cut it off.

CHARLES. While I was sleeping.

NORAH. His mother and I had a great big laugh about it and she finally liked me. Which was great 'til I got pregnant and then she became so overbearing –

CHARLES. No she wasn't.

NORAH. I didn't want her to like me anymore. But by the way he reacted, you woulda thought I cut off a lot more than just his ponytail. He threw a tantrum, he was crying –

CHARLES. I wasn't crying.

NORAH. He didn't get out of bed for two days.

CHARLES. No.

NORAH. Cuz his ponytail made him feel like a young artist again, *(To him.)* didn't it? Full of verve on the cusp of something great instead of being a chubby middle-aged man looking back at what could've been if you were only man enough to pursue it! Oh, did that hurt? You need Ms. Nora now to make you feel like a man? *(To audience.)* What?! You don't know everything. He made me feel guilty for buying five maternity jeans while I was pregnant and constantly teased me about getting fat. *(To him.)* I wasn't getting fat, I was making a baby, you idiot!

CHARLES. You're right. Ms. Nora does makes me feel like a man. She does. She also makes Mountain feel safe and loved. And she will be his prime example of womanhood for the rest of his life cuz you needed to go back to work to feel like you were good at something.

(She looks away. He looks away.)

NORAH. *(Almost a whisper.)* What's wrong with us?

CHARLES. What?

NORAH. *(Beat.)* What's wrong with us?

CHARLES. *(Beat.)* We don't know how to talk to each other.

NORAH. I tried. You walked out.

CHARLES. Asking me about dates?! If I'm free?! That's your idea of –

NORAH. Fine! You want the food truck? You can have your Filipino Food Truck to play with. But it's gonna be Nora spelled with an "H"! *(Beat.)* Play me the song. Play me your song, Charles. I wanna hear it.

CHARLES. No.

NORAH. It's the money my mother left me after she died. Play me your stupid song or no food truck.

CHARLES. You know what's wrong with us? You don't hear me cuz you're always thinking about what you're gonna say next so you look good in front of them.

NORAH. Just to be clear, you asked what's wrong with <u>us</u>, and it's my fault?

CHARLES. My point exactly.

NORAH. I don't care about them.

CHARLES. Yes you do.

NORAH. Say something worth hearing and I'm all ears.

CHARLES. I hate my job.

NORAH. Then quit.

CHARLES. And whenever I mention it, you dismiss it. *(Imitating* **NORAH**.*)* "It's called 'work,' Charles, cuz it takes work. Welcome to adulthood!" *(To audience.)* That's verbatim.

NORAH. If you're not happy, do something about it. I'm not responsible for your happiness.

CHARLES. Of course you are.

NORAH. No, I'm not. I have my life and you have yours.

CHARLES. Then what the fuck is a marriage?! What are we doing here?! Of course you're responsible for me! I'm responsible for you! We make each other!

NORAH. You're blaming me for the disappointment you feel with your life?

CHARLES. Yes! And you blame me for yours.

NORAH. No, I don't.

CHARLES. You're just saying that for them.

NORAH. I don't care about them!

CHARLES. Were you upset that I bought this bed without talking to you about it –

NORAH. Yes.

CHARLES. Or! ...Were you upset that I bought this bed without talking to you about it <u>in front of them</u>? Cuz of how it made you look?! Like, you had no say in anything between us even though that's totally not true. If they weren't here, I guarantee you, it wouldn't've been a problem. But what they think of you, their opinion of you, the kind of woman you appear to be in their eyes matters so much to you, you just couldn't let it go and had to make a big mess of it all.

NORAH. *(Beat.)* Don't answer right away.

CHARLES. About what?

NORAH. I'm gonna ask you a question and even if you know the answer right away, don't answer. And if you don't know the answer right away, take the time to think about it. Either way, I won't know if you had a ready answer or if you're thinking about it cuz you're not gonna answer right away. Nod your head if you understand.

CHARLES. See? "Nod your head if you understand." That was for them.

NORAH. Well, "That's verbatim," was all for them too.

CHARLES. Fine, ask your question and I'll answer right away.

NORAH. No. You're <u>not</u> gonna answer right away!

CHARLES. I just said the wrong thing! What's your question?

NORAH. *(Takes a breath.)* Most couples don't last. My parents got a divorce, Kate and her partner split up, Dale and his wife aren't doing too well.

CHARLES. Who's Dale?

NORAH. Point is, it's not ideal but people figure it out and they move on. We can still be Mountain's parents and not be together. But we can't keep doing this.

CHARLES. Ask your question.

NORAH. And don't answer right away. *(Looks away.)* Do you still love me? *(A long pause.)* Okay. That's long enough. What's your answer?

CHARLES. *(A bit detached.)* Yes, I do. Do you still love me? I don't need you to take a pause, unless you need to.

NORAH. No. *(Beat.)* No, I don't...need a pause. *(A bit detached.)* Yes. I still love you.

CHARLES. Then why are we so mean to each other?

NORAH. I don't know.

CHARLES. *(Beat.)* Maybe a vacation is what we need. We're always better when we're not here. Maybe we should just vacation for the rest of our lives.

NORAH. I think we should see a marriage counselor.

CHARLES. Why'd you hire Ms. Nora? Hm?

NORAH. Cuz I wanted more for Mountain.

CHARLES. Than me?

NORAH. Than me. *(Beat.)* I don't have good mom skills. I don't know how other moms do it.

CHARLES. *(Beat.)* They ask for help. At the drop-in centre they do. And I think you think asking for help makes you look weak but it actually makes you generous cuz it raises the status of the person you're asking. *(Beat.)* I got that from a TED Talk.

NORAH. You're right. You are. But you're also not here.

CHARLES. We're kind of in a good place right now maybe we shouldn't –

NORAH. I don't ask you for help also because you're bothered by anything to do with Mountain.

CHARLES. That's not true.

NORAH. You're great playing with him but when he starts crying you get so frustrated so fast.

CHARLES. So do you.

NORAH. I know. I'm not –

CHARLES. I had a bad dad, I became a bad dad.

NORAH. That's your excuse?

CHARLES. That's my reason.

NORAH. To justify your behaviour?

CHARLES. No, to understand it. Why I'm so bad at this. Why I don't feel like a dad.

NORAH. Why do you have to feel like one? He makes you one.

CHARLES. He doesn't want me as his dad.

NORAH. He said that to you?

CHARLES. He keeps pushing me away. There's no connection.

NORAH. Then make one. Do that firetruck jigsaw puzzle with him every day for a week and by the end of the week, you'll have a firetruck jigsaw puzzle connection guaranteed. You'll have a good shared memory. That's what we're doing now!

CHARLES. You're telling me this?!

NORAH. *(This hits her really hard.)* You're right. I have no authority to advise you on parenting whatsoever but yes, I am telling you this and not because I think I'm better than you but because I love you and Mountain so much and want what's best for you both. That's it. Keep pursuing him, Charles, and he'll make you into the man, the dad you fear you won't ever become.

CHARLES. *(Long beat.)* This is good.

NORAH. What?

CHARLES. This.

NORAH. Talking?

CHARLES. Yeah. We should do it more often.

NORAH. *(Beat.)* Can I hear your song now?

CHARLES. *(Beat. Sings a cappella*.)*
WHERE DO YOU GO WHEN YOU WANT CHICKEN ADOBO
AFTER THAT BIG GIG WHERE CAN YOU GET SISIG
WE'RE ON THE ROAD, NOT FAR FROM YOU
WE'RE LIKE MEALS ON WHEELS BUT WITH FILIPINO FOOD

NORA'S FILIPINO FOOD TRUCK *(Clap clap.)*
NORA'S FILIPINO FOOD TRUCK *(Clap clap.)*
NORA'S FILIPINO FOOD TRUCK *(Clap clap.)*

IN YOUR NEIGHBOURHOOD WITH FILIPINO FOOD.
IT'S GOOD LUCK TO EAT AT NORA'S FILIPINO FOOD TRUCK

NORAH. I meant the recording.

*(**CHARLES** goes to get the recording.)*

It's okay. I'll get a friend to crunch the numbers and suss out the possibilities.

CHARLES. About the food truck?

NORAH. Yeah. It's a good song, Charles.

CHARLES. *(Re: audience.)* What do we do about them?

(Beat. It's like they're starting the play over, more conscious of how they make each other.)

---

* A license to produce *Bad Parent* does not include a performance license for any third-party or copyrighted music. Licensees should create an original composition or use music in the public domain. For further information, please see the Music and Third-Party Materials Use Note on page iii.

NORAH. We first met at Kate's wedding. Kate invited me. We were closer back then.

CHARLES. I was actually working the wedding. Part of the serving staff. In between jobs. Kinda aimless really. I served her a drink.

NORAH. He looked cute in his little bow tie.

CHARLES. She was the most beautiful woman at the wedding. She was constantly surrounded by really attractive, buff guys.

NORAH. Who were all gay.

CHARLES. Which I didn't know at the time.

NORAH. He presumed I had ordered the drink.

CHARLES. I really thought she did.

NORAH. I went along with it and then we started talking about yoga. I was into hot yoga back then.

CHARLES. She was.

NORAH. He thought hot yoga was where hot-looking people did yoga.

CHARLES. I was joking. It was a move.

NORAH. It worked.

CHARLES. She spoke with elegance and smart-ness. I was just trying not to mess up.

NORAH. He invited me to a gig.

CHARLES. I did.

NORAH. He told me he was an artist.

CHARLES. And she believed me.

NORAH. I don't remember what else happened at that wedding but I didn't care.

CHARLES. I got fired cuz I spent too much time with her but I didn't care either. She was worth it. And then she got me a job. And helped me get my life in order.

NORAH. And then we got married.

CHARLES. Had a baby.

NORAH. And now we're trying not to be bad parents.

CHARLES. *(Mountain cries. To her.)* I'll get him.

NORAH. Let him cry it out.

CHARLES. You sure?

NORAH. *(Beat.)* No.

> *(They both listen to the cry of Mountain that increases. They both consider heading over at different times. They look at each other. They look at the audience. Snap to black.)*

The End

Some Thoughts About the Play

This is a play about a married couple dealing with dormant marital issues that surface once they have a baby. It's also about inherited parenting practices and the crippling pressures social media or any audience, real or imagined, creates in how we parent and how we treat our spouse. It's also about making public what has been experienced in private; the public discourse of real marriage issues. It's also a clown show.

The music of the text happens when there's a bit of pace to the scenes. Not rushed but earning the beats and silences.

Charles and Norah are exhausted and frustrated. There's a fatigued intensity to them.

I wrote the songs but any sound designer can mess with it. The food truck song should sound cute and made on a simple recording software like Garageband. The initial recording of *Run Norah Run* should sound like it was roughly done on Voice Memos on a phone, but the concert version should sound similar to the bands Metric, Chvrches and Japanese Breakfast.

The following three poems were written while I wrote this play. They are spiritually connected and I felt compelled to include them here. These are poems to myself, poems I needed to hear, and I hope they benefit you too.

– Ins Choi

Get Started

Get started
Get started before you get hard hearted
Get started before your dearly beloved becomes dearly departed
Start it
I know it's hard
Starting is hard
It's hard to start
It might be the hardest part
Starting
From nothing to something
Something from nothing
Cuz you can do something with something
Something can be done if there's something there
But nothing's nothing
It's a different thing
It's a lack of a thing
It's no thing
What do you do with no thing?
What can you do?
Nothing
There's nothing you can do with nothing
But order another coffee
Check another email
Scratch another sensible itch
And as offence turns to defence
Creation turns to maintenance
And bam
Nothing's back
But once you start
Just like that
Nothing's gone
That taunting void is silenced
The spell is broken and the despairing abyss of a blank page urging you to relent, vanishes
And don't worry, craft will come later
Yes, rigour will come later
I promise you, rhythm, rhyme, reason will all come later
But for now, no matter how bad that plot is
Or if the horse is in front of where the cart is
Know your supple heart is where your start is and get started

Not Too Much

Not too much
Just enough
Less
Way less
What are you doing?
Just suggest it, right?
Don't rob the audience of their role
Come on, you're not delivering a message efficiently here
That's not what's happening
It's not about making sure everyone's on board
You're not force feeding anybody
But you're not taking off either
Cuz it's not for you
It's for them
Don't forget that
You're doing this for them cuz you love them
And you're almost there
I know you've been almost there for a long time but stop now and it's a poorly told story
That's not a threat nor a denial of how hard this is
In fact, if I'm coming off sounding a bit too cavalier, it's perhaps a touch of despair at the near impossibility of telling a story well that's flavouring my voice
The rule is a story poorly told
That's what usually happens cuz poorly told stories don't care who you are, or how much you've invested
They're brazen survivors that fear no one and fight tooth and nail to exist on your page arrogantly confident that you'll tire and give up
Whereas, a story well told is that rare invitation, that purifying fire that awakens us to where we were going and why
The world needs your story
And your story needs you to tell it well
Don't give up
You're almost there
Love them
I know you do

I Think It's Time to Let Go

I think it's time to let go
Time to magnify something else
What do you think?
I know
It's been a comforting return
Here
These pages
A familiar place to go to no matter how you feel, where what you do is immensely appreciated by your future self, I'm with ya
It's also something to hold onto, right? a footing, when things get a bit slippy, leaving each time knowing you'll return to find it hasn't changed at all since the last draft
It stayed exactly the same after so much in your life shifted
Or you return pleasantly surprised at all the revisions only to realize it was you at three in the morning grasping at a phrase you dreamt about or a turn in the story you woke up to write down immediately cuz it was the fix for that wrong you couldn't see when you were awake

And so many times you thought you were done, I know
But now it's time for you to let go

Of course they may hate it or not care
And yes, you will be found out
You will be known
But it's not for you, remember, it's for them

So
Ready?
Raise your arm
Go ahead
Go on, raise it   *(Extend an arm with a tight fist.)*
Nice and easy
Good
And now one finger at a time   *(Slowly open the fist.)*
There you go
Keep going
You're almost there
That's it
Mm hm   *(Fingers stretch out. Exhale.)*
Well done

www.ingramcontent.com/pod-product-compliance
Lightning Source LLC
Chambersburg PA
CBHW072021290426
44109CB00018B/2307